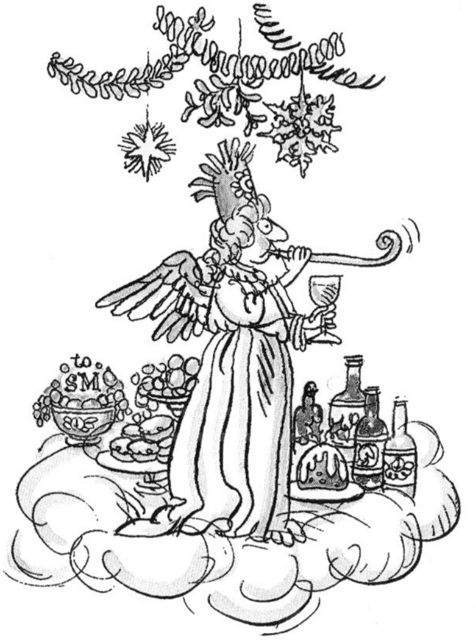
to
SM

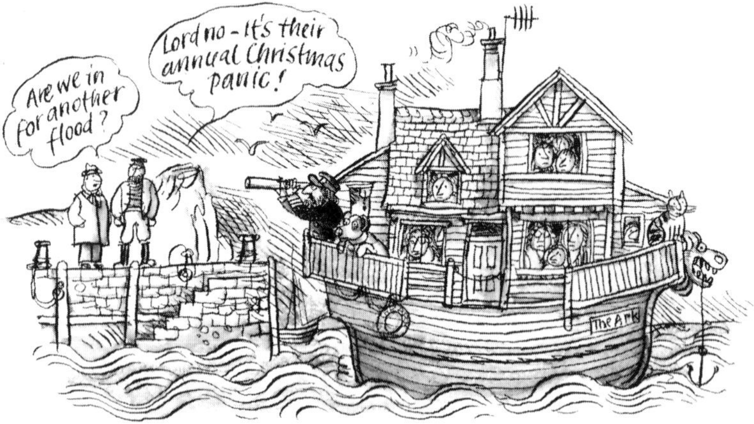
Are we in for another flood?
Lord no - It's their annual Christmas panic!
The Ark

Don't look now
but it's Christmas again!

Fritz
wegner

Patrick Hardy Books

PATRICK HARDY BOOKS
28 Percy Street, London
W1P 9FF, UK.

Copyright text and
illustrations © 1983
by Fritz Wegner

First published in 1983

Printed in Great Britain
By W.S. COWELL LTD
IPSWICH.

HARDBACK ISBN : 07444 0006 6
PAPERBACK ISBN: 07444 00017 1

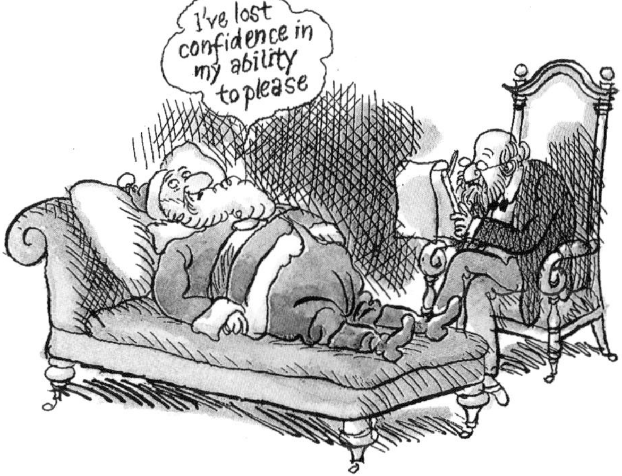
I've lost confidence in my ability to please

Further cutbacks were announced by
the Oecumenical Council of Christmas cheer

Fancy a sizzling good time, darling?

I would like to know what sign he is following!

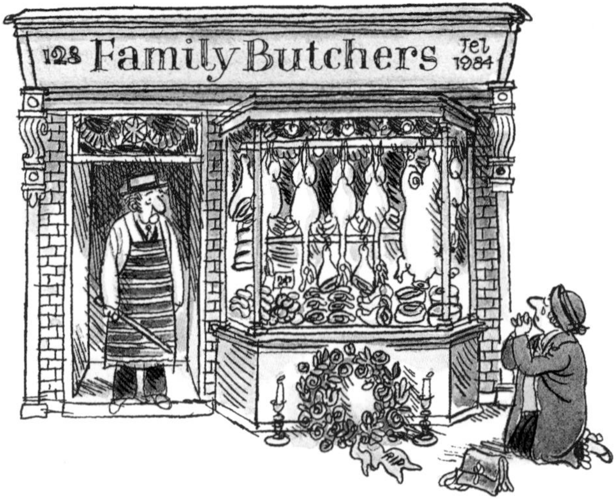
128 Family Butchers Tel 1984

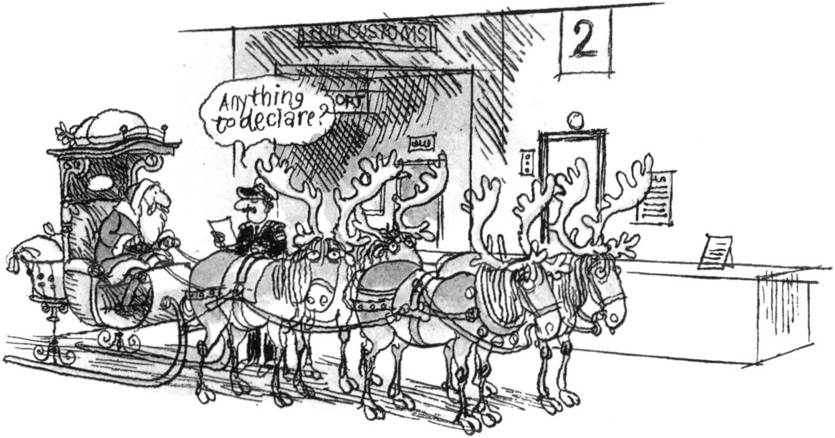
Anything to declare?
2

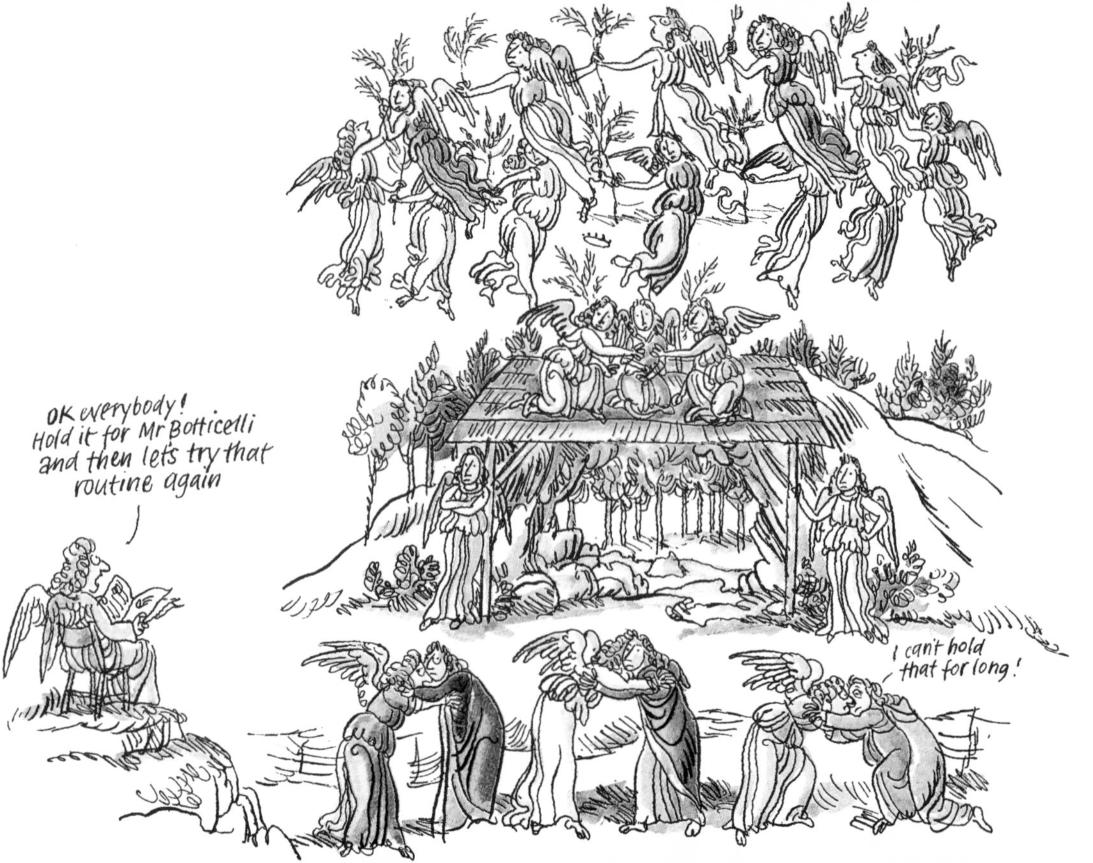
OK everybody!
Hold it for Mr Botticelli
and then let's try that
routine again
I can't hold
that for long!

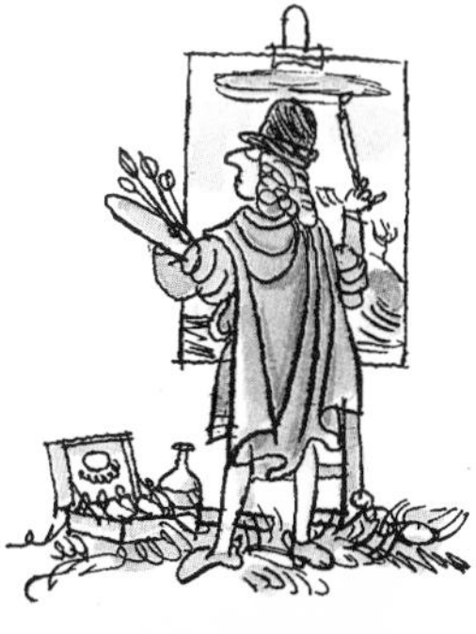

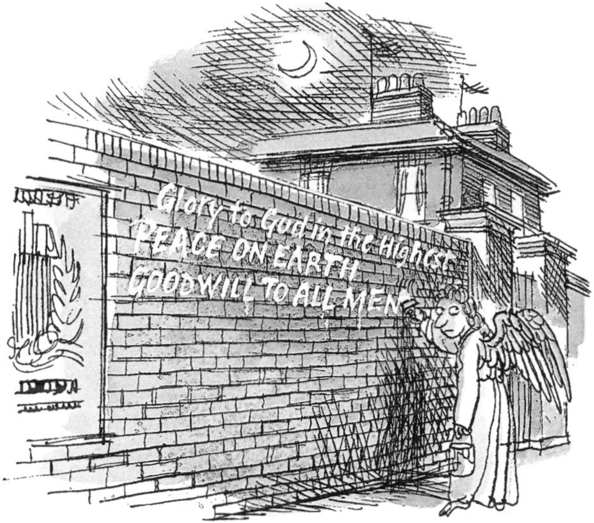
Glory to God in the Highest
PEACE ON EARTH
GOODWILL TO ALL MEN

*Glory to God in the Highest - Peace on Earth,
Goodwill to all men!*

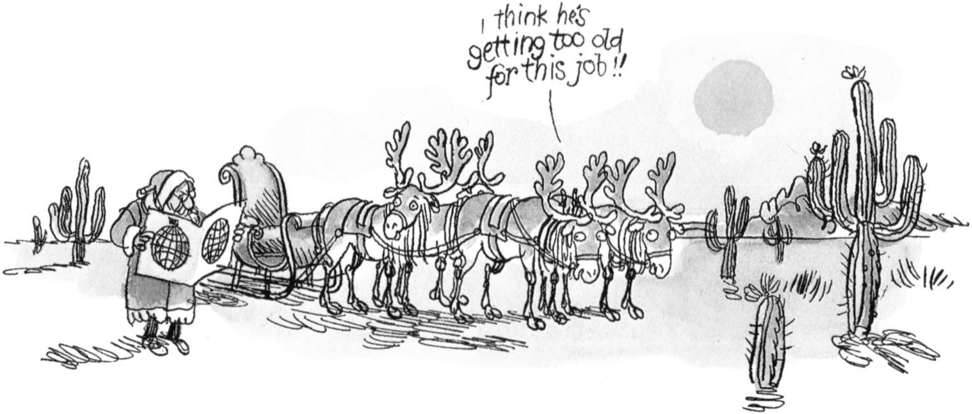
I think he's getting too old for this job!!

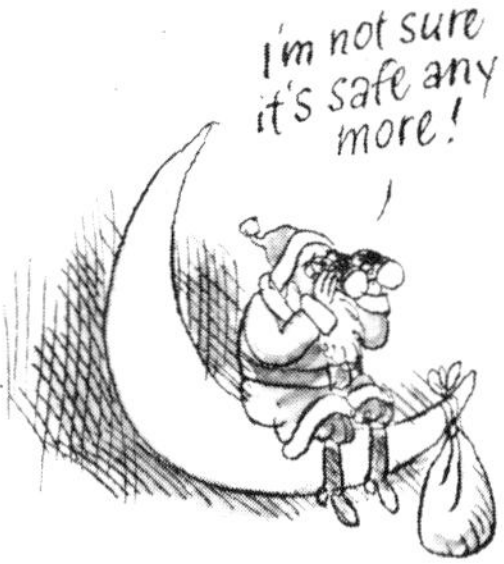
I'm not sure it's safe any more!

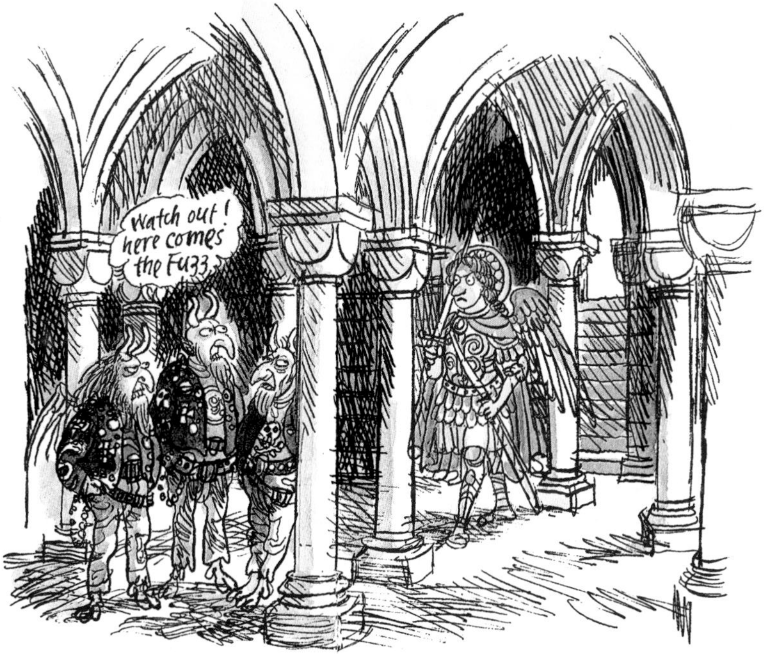
Watch out! here comes the Fuzz

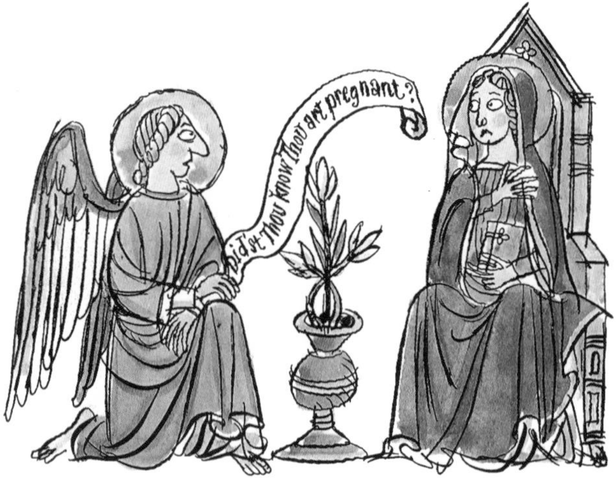
Did'st Thou know Thou art pregnant?

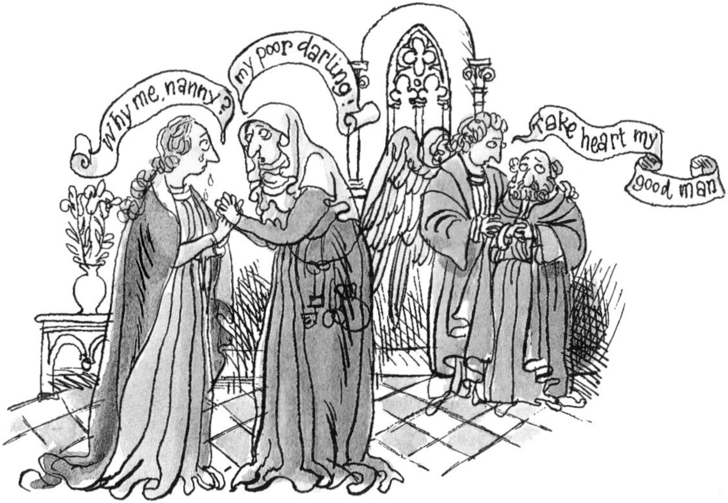
why me, nanny?
my poor darling!
Take heart my good man

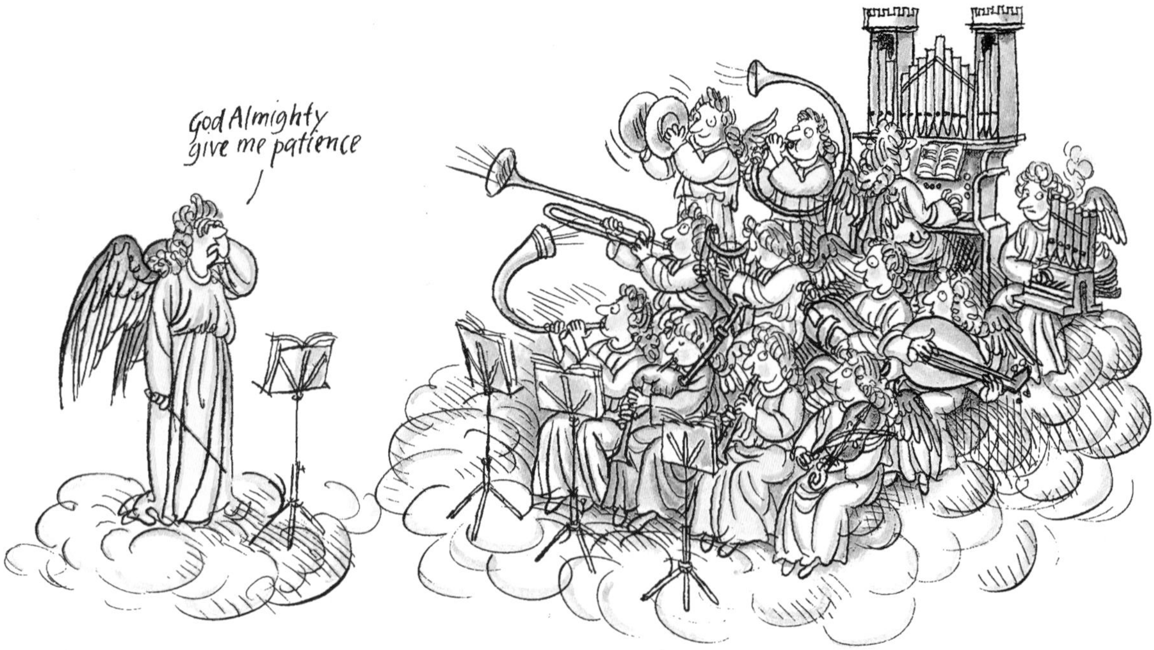
God Almighty
give me patience

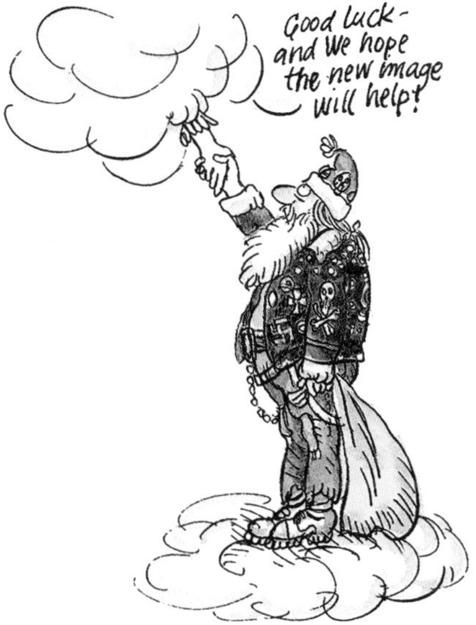
Good luck -
and we hope
the new image
will help!

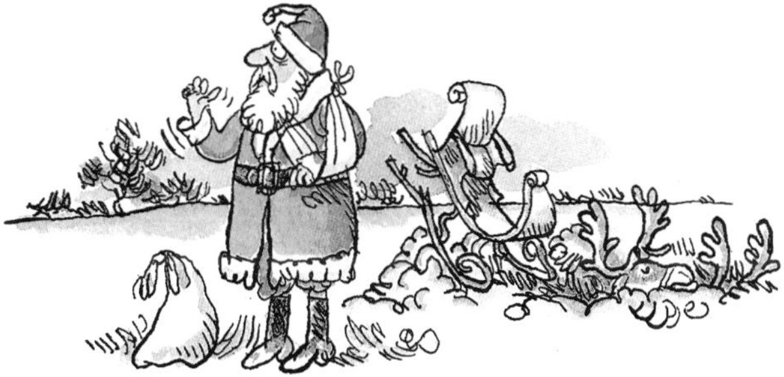

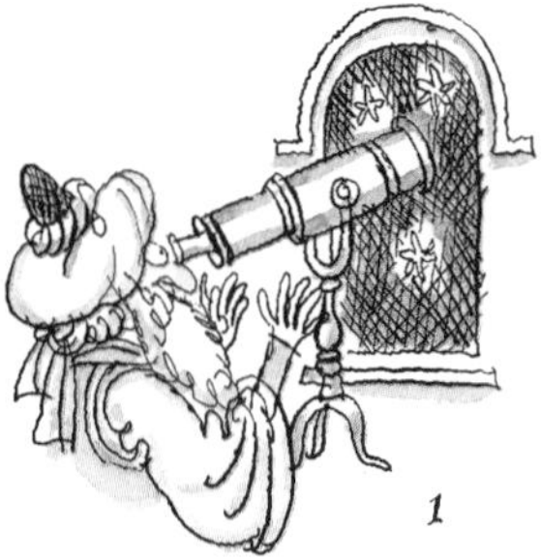

1

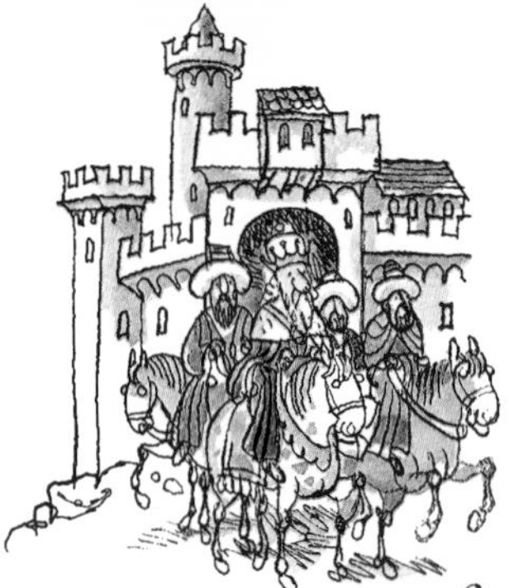

2

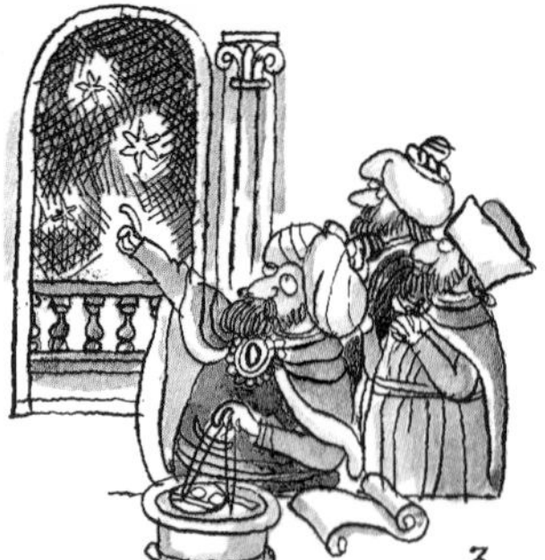

3

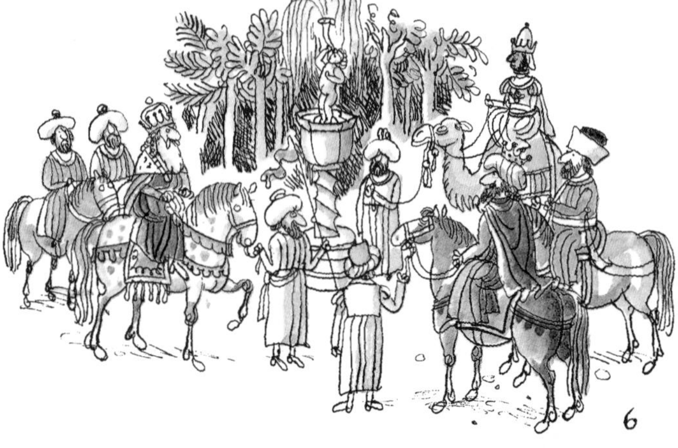

6

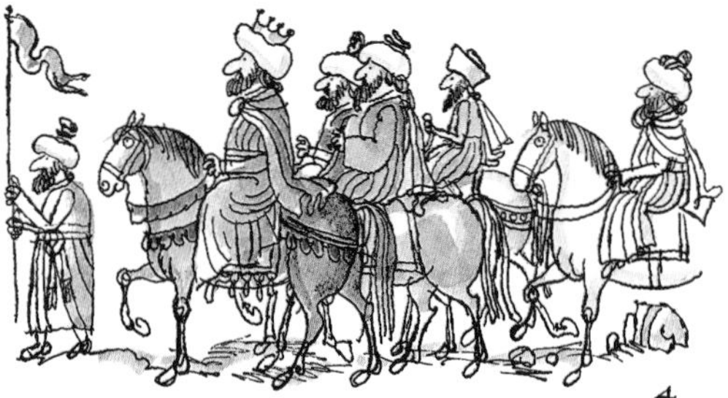

4

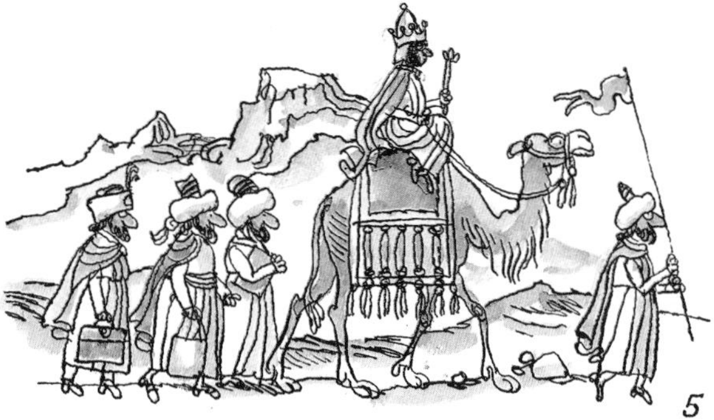

5

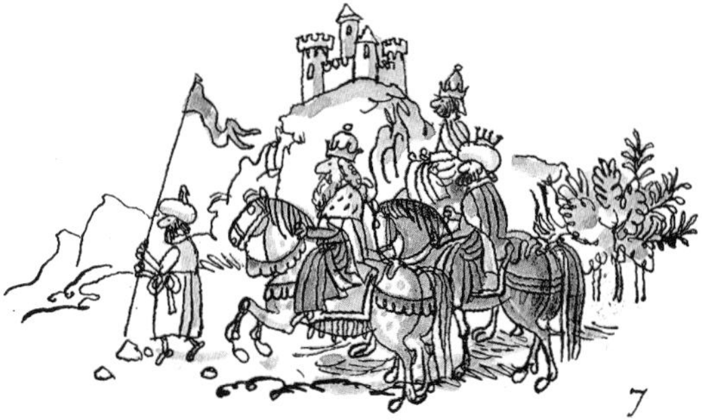

7

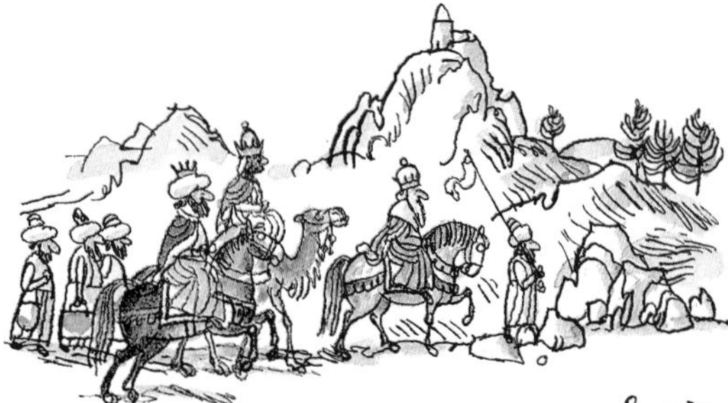

8 →

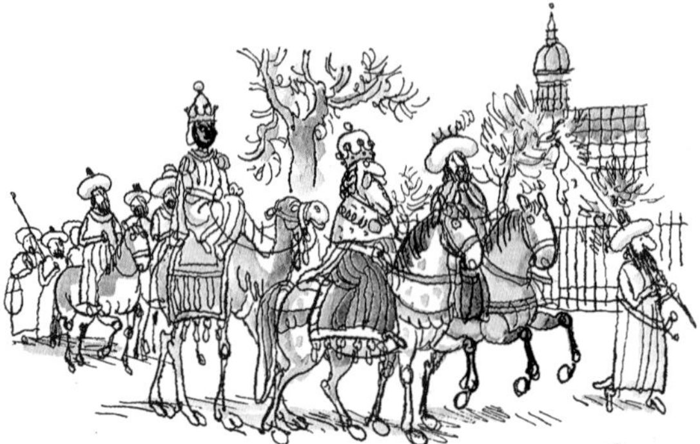

9

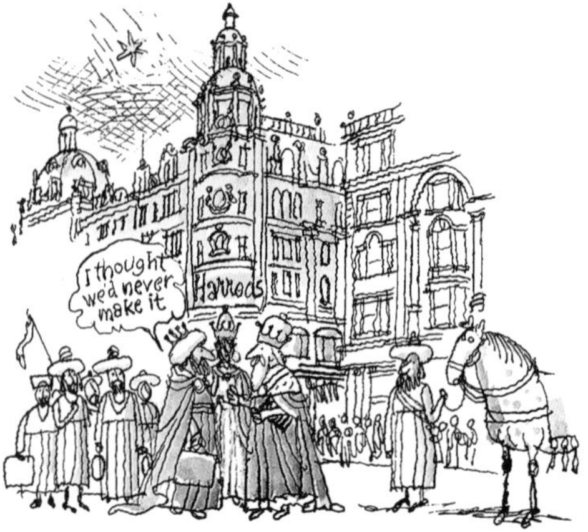

I thought we'd never make it
Harrods

10

"They've always got to go one better than the rest!

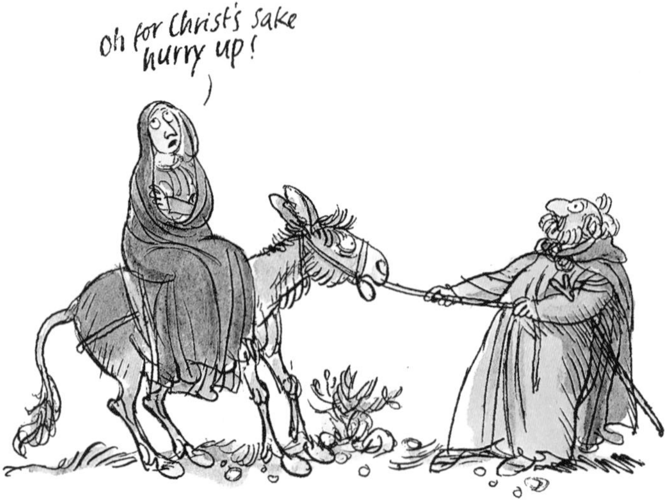
Oh for Christ's sake hurry up!

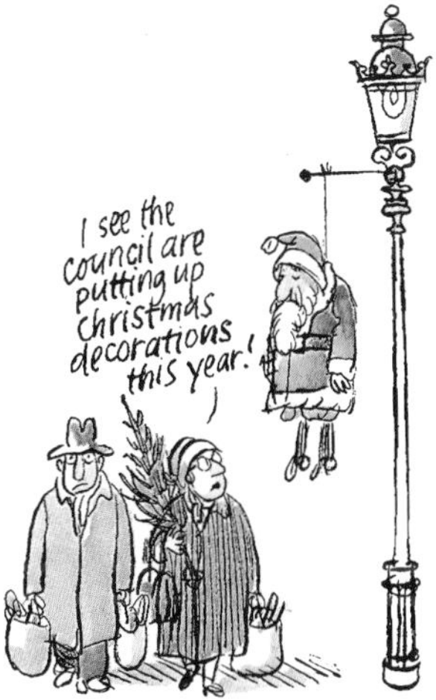
I see the council are putting up christmas decorations this year!

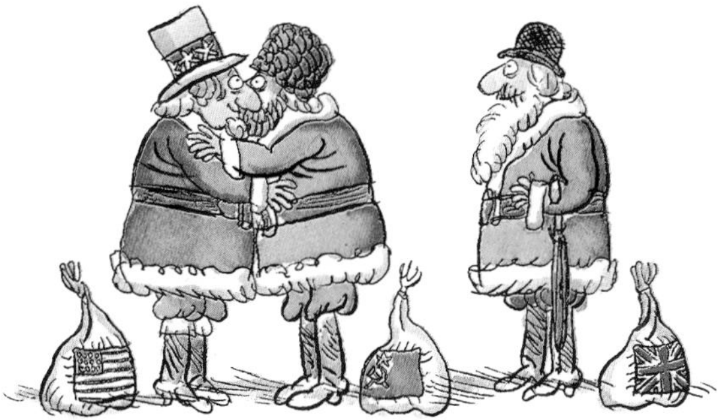

Entente cordiale

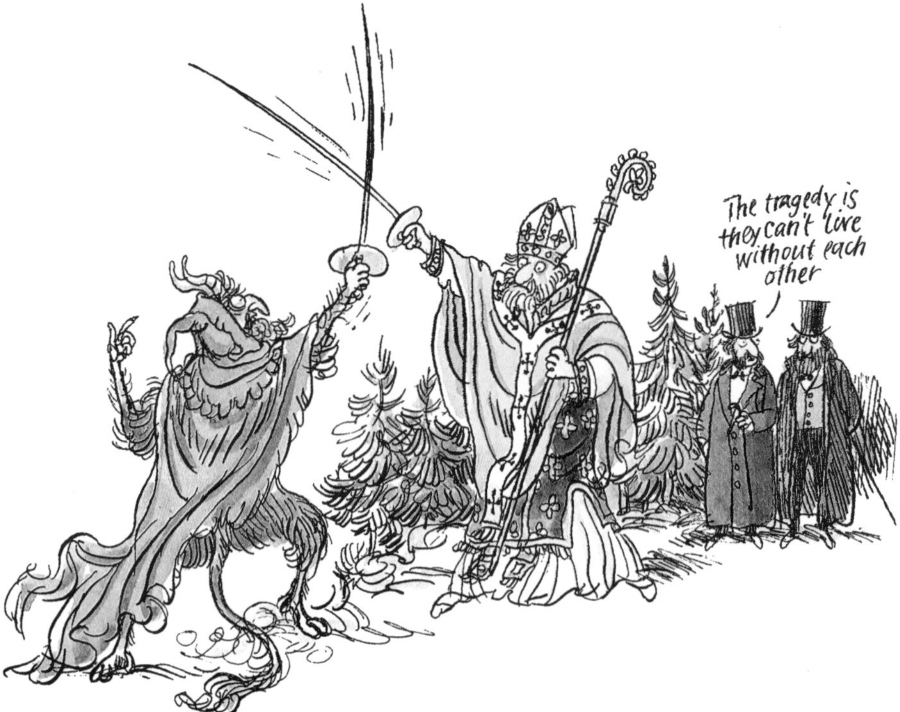
The tragedy is they can't live without each other

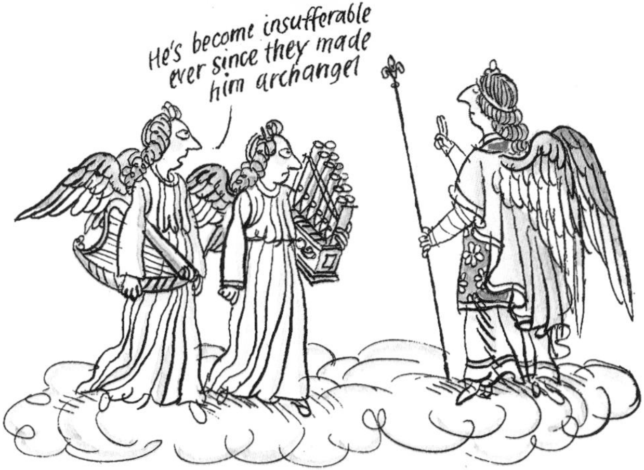
He's become insufferable ever since they made him archangel

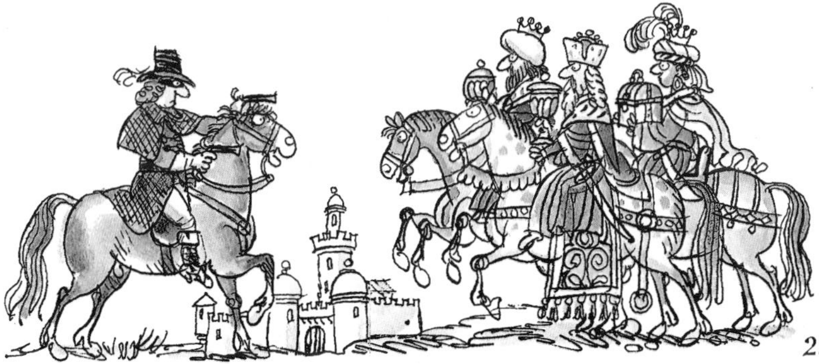

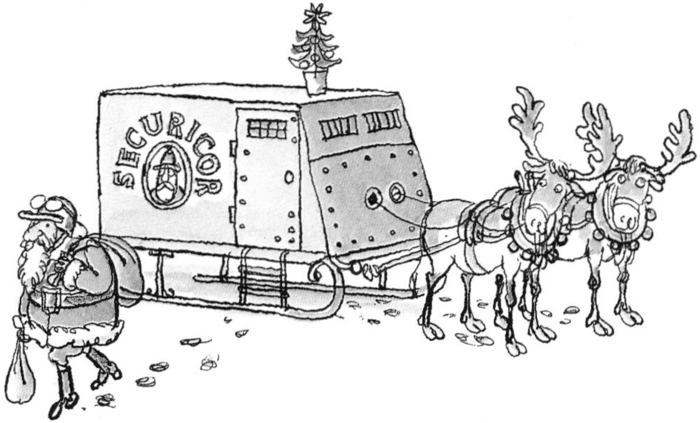
SECURICOR

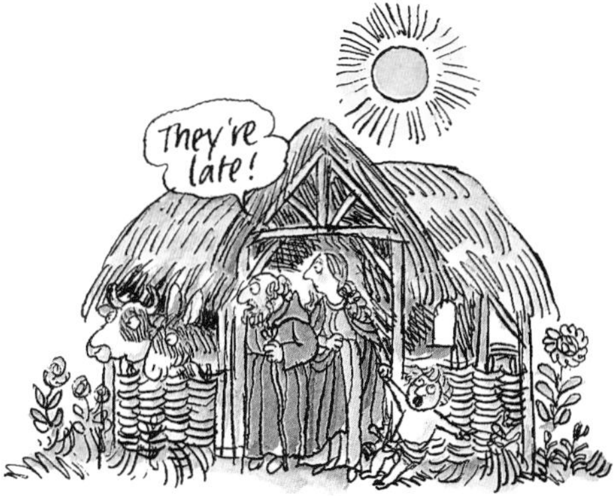
They're late!

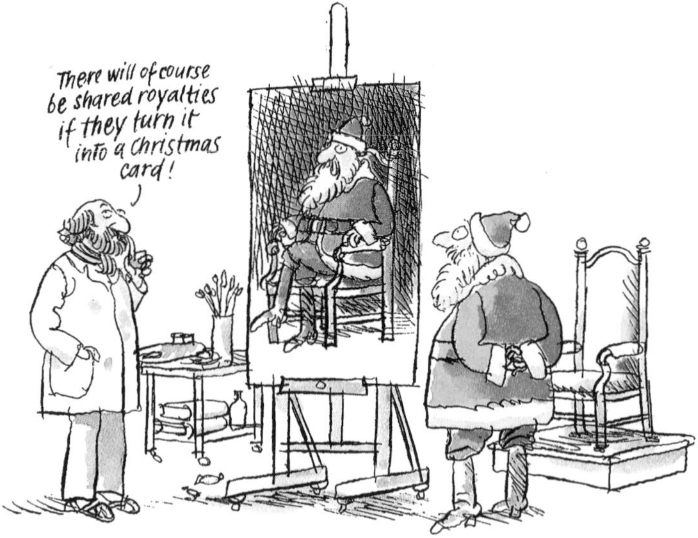
There will of course be shared royalties if they turn it into a Christmas card!

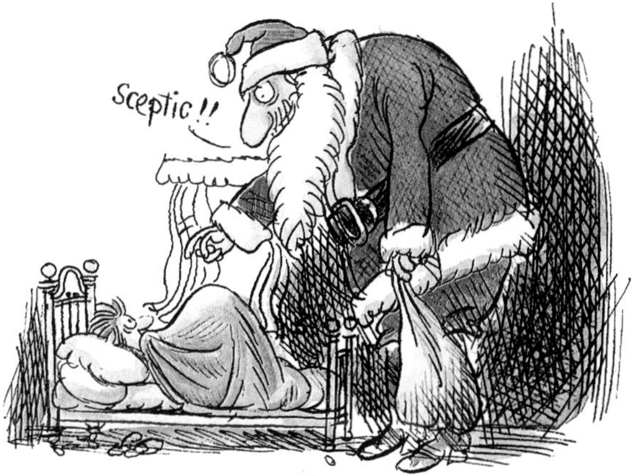
Sceptic !!

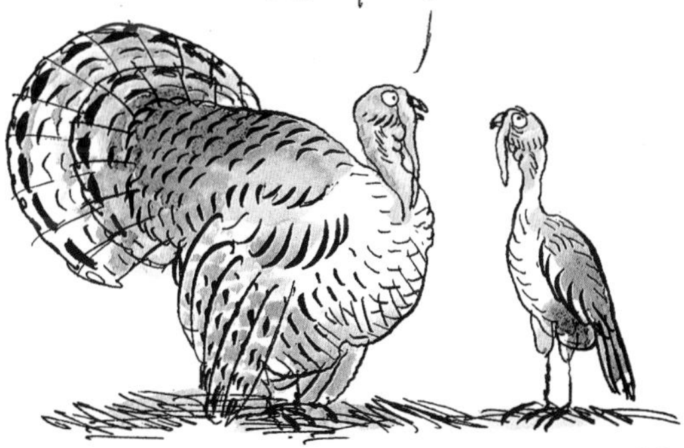
If you want to make the Christmas table you'd better put a bit of weight on !

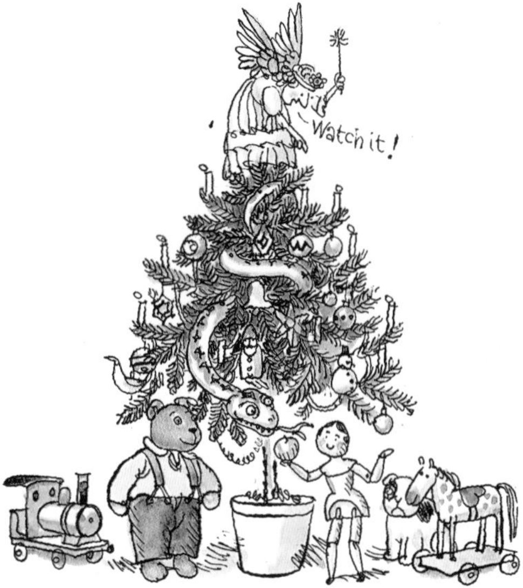
Watch it!

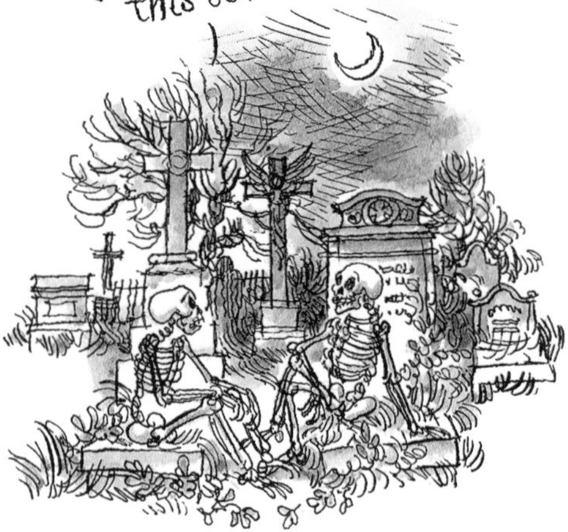
I just can't work up any Christmas spirit this season

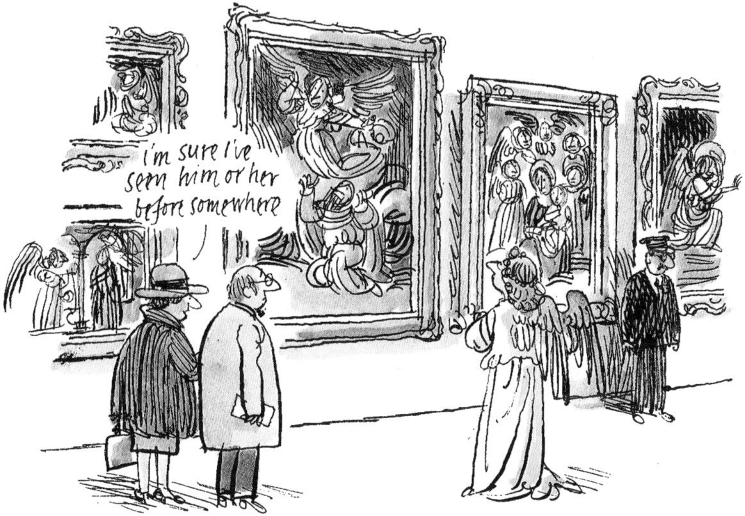
I'm sure I've seen him or her before somewhere

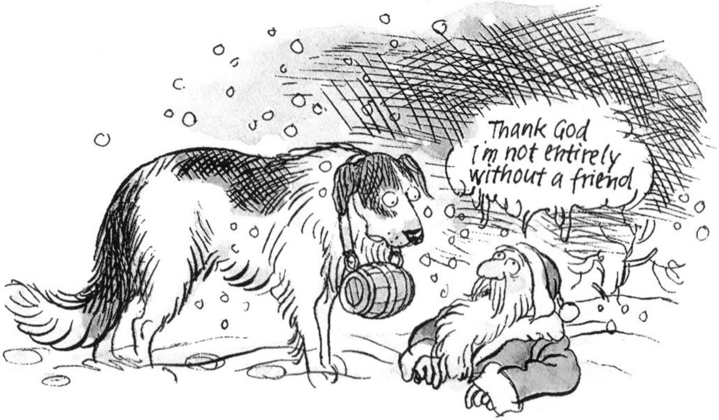
Thank God I'm not entirely without a friend

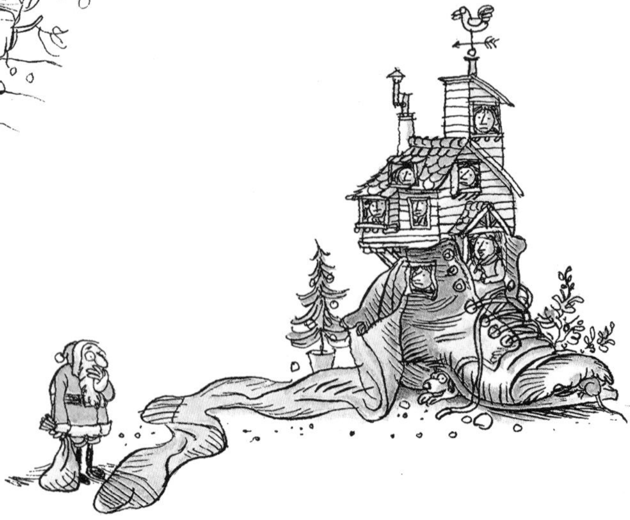

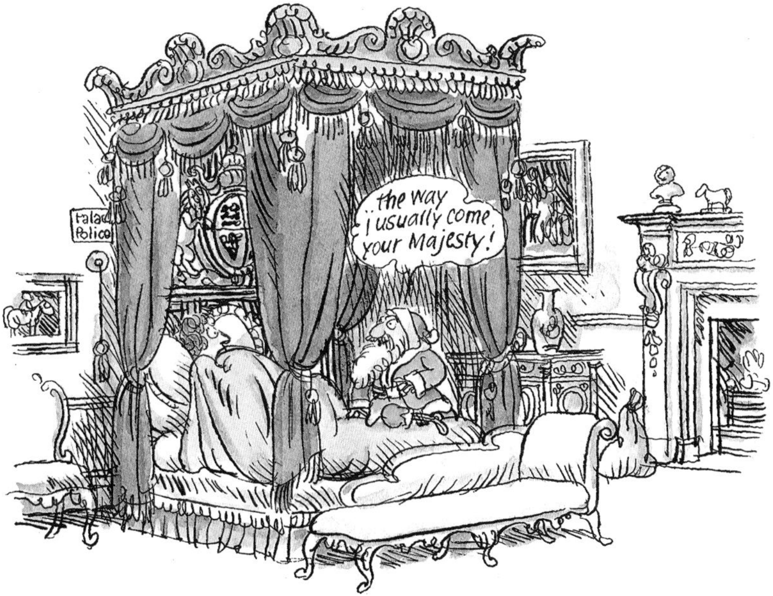
the way i usually come your Majesty!
Police

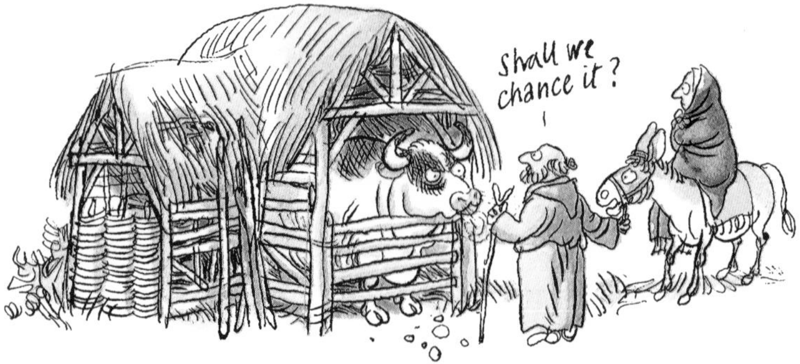
Shall we chance it?

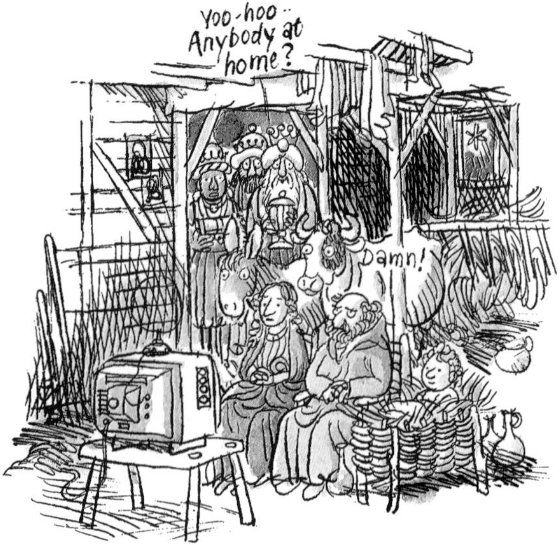
Yoo-hoo.. Anybody at home?
Damn!

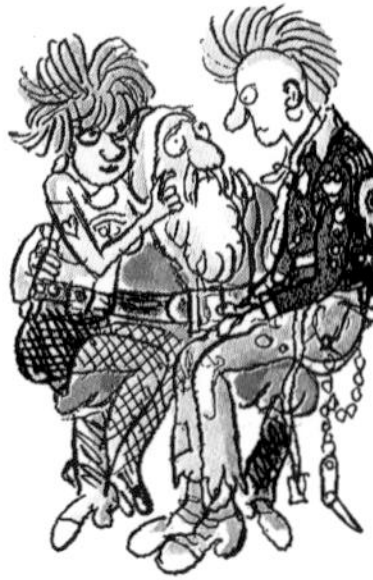

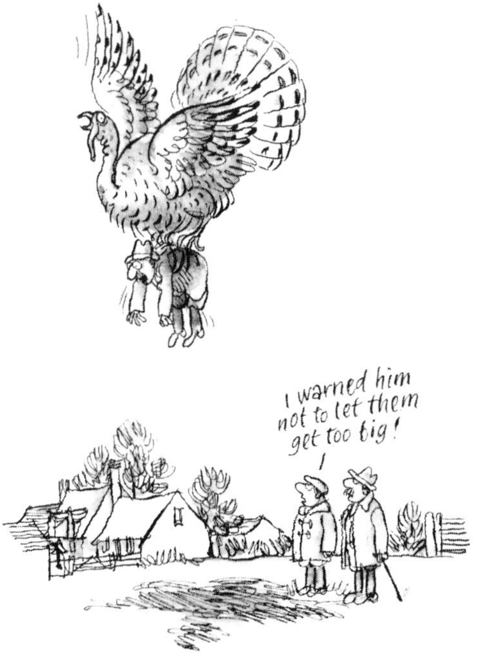
I warned him not to let them get too big!

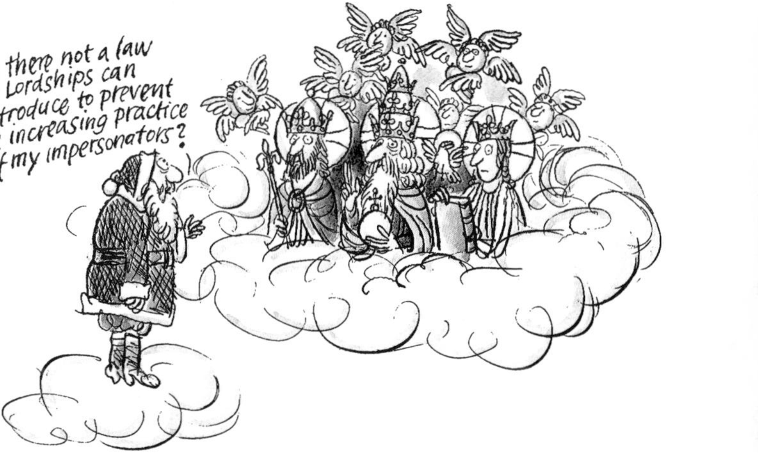
Is there not a law your Lordships can introduce to prevent the increasing practice of my impersonators?

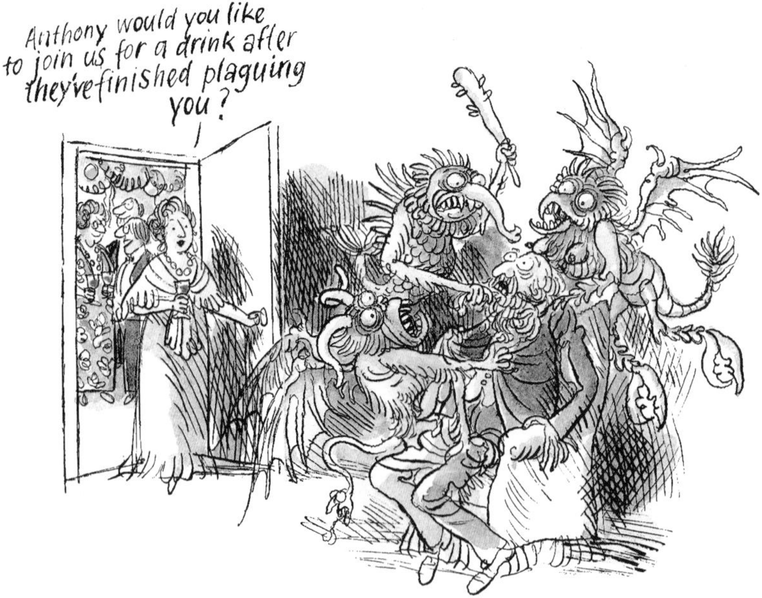
Anthony would you like to join us for a drink after they've finished plaguing you?

The Temptation of St. Anthony

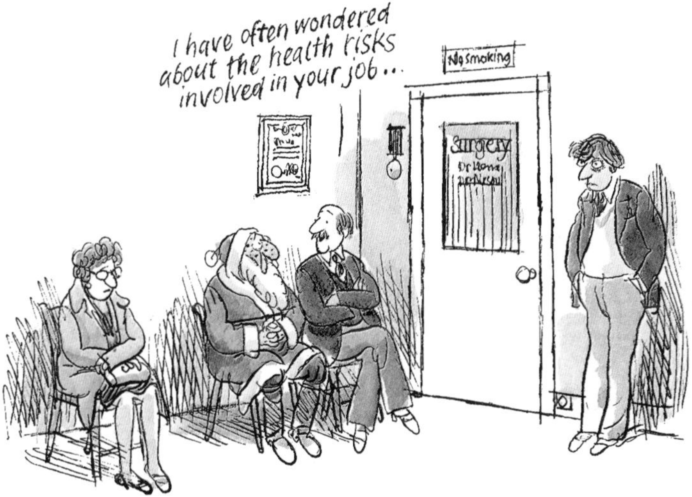
I have often wondered about the health risks involved in your job...
No smoking
Surgery

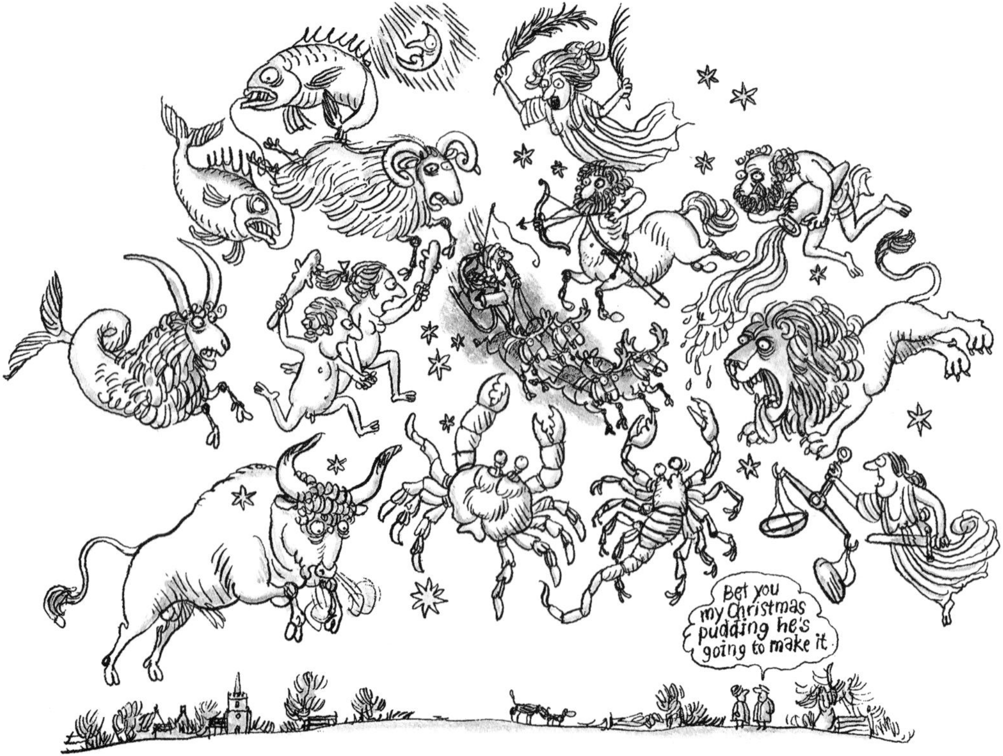
Bet you my Christmas pudding he's going to make it.

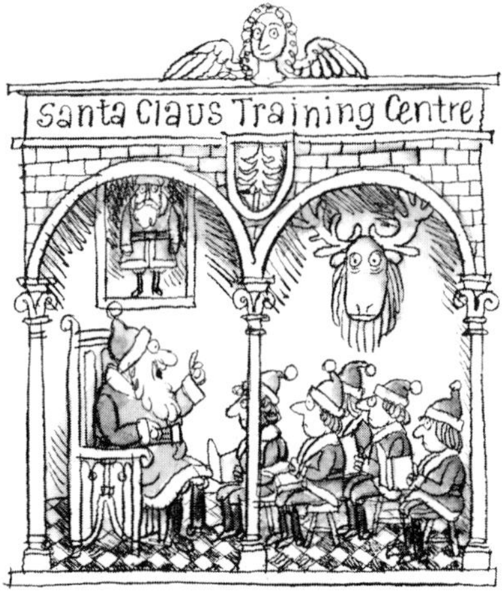
Santa Claus Training Centre

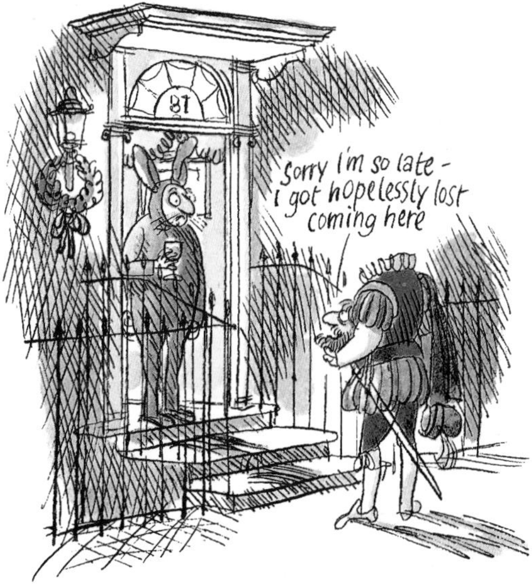
81
Sorry I'm so late - I got hopelessly lost coming here

He's getting more extravagant each Christmas

We actually managed to find something to please Henry this Christmas!

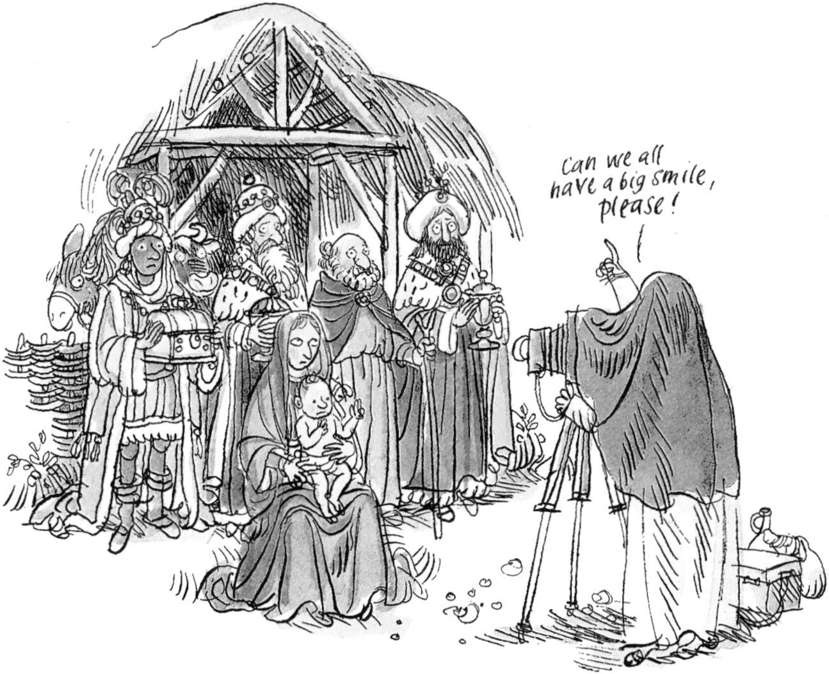
Can we all have a big smile, please!

1

2

3

44

4

5

6

Help!!

7

8

9

10

11 →

12

13

Love and Peace
with thee abide
Through the
holy
Christmas tide.

14

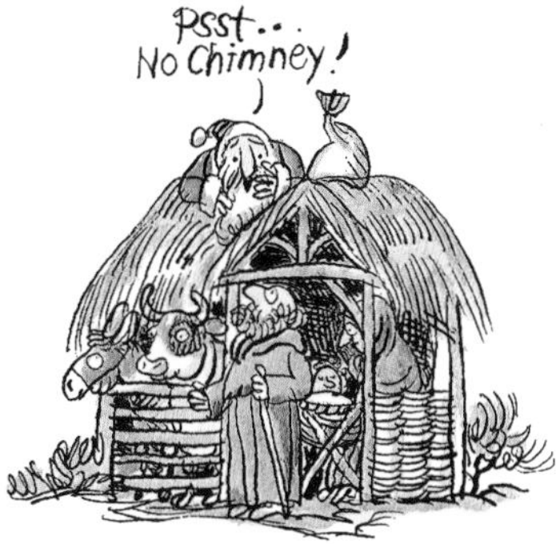
Psst...
No Chimney!

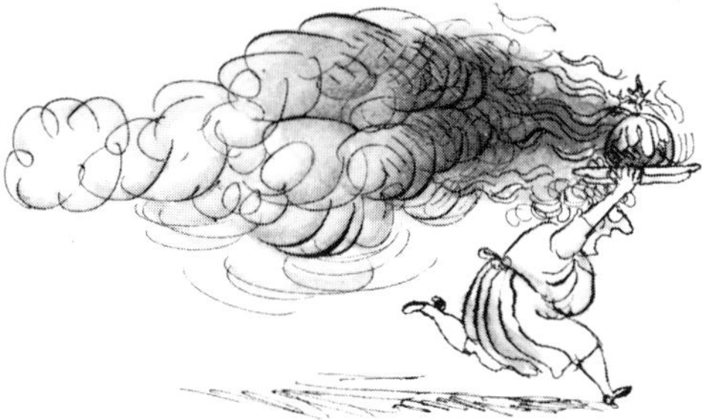

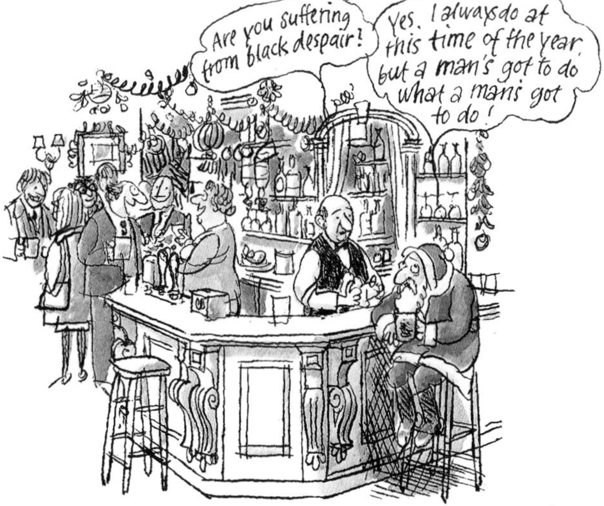
Are you suffering from black despair?
Yes. I always do at this time of the year, but a man's got to do what a man's got to do!

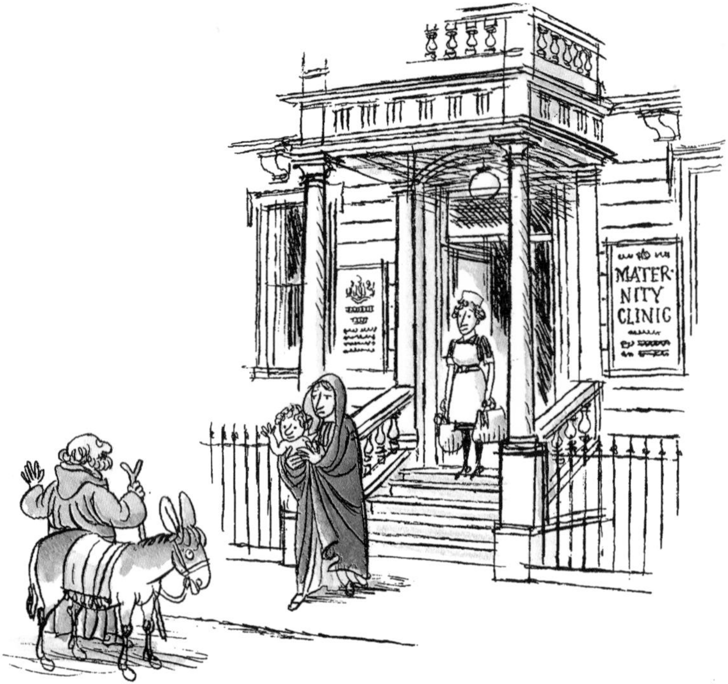
MATER-
NITY
CLINIC

49

Welcome Presents

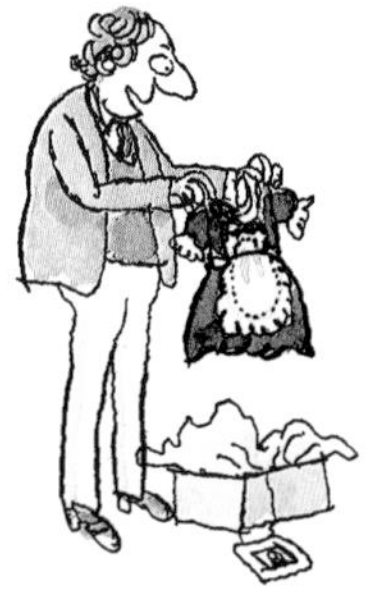

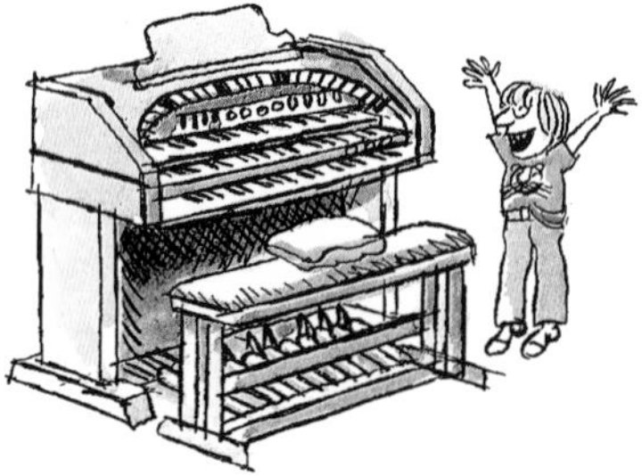

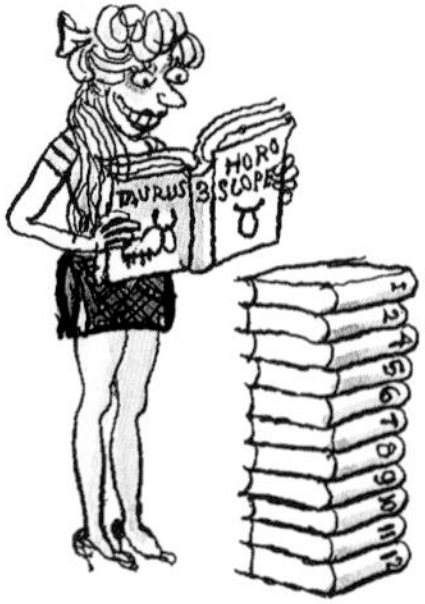
TAURUS
HORO SCOPE

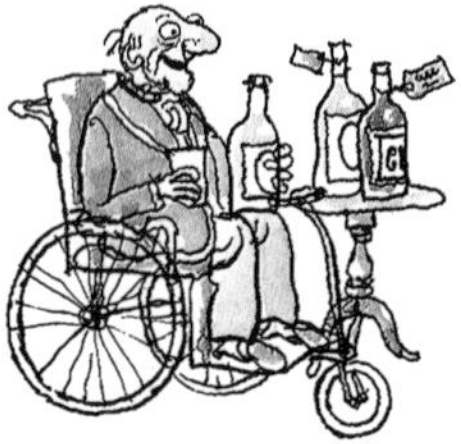

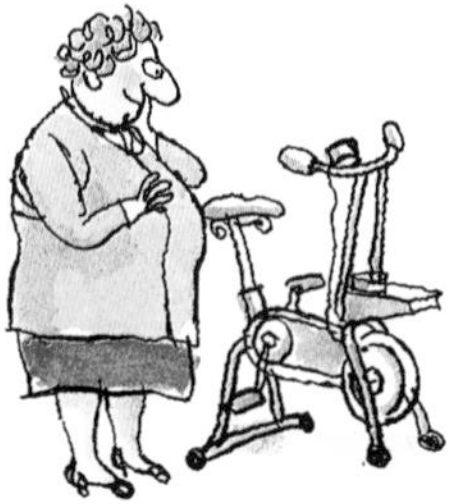

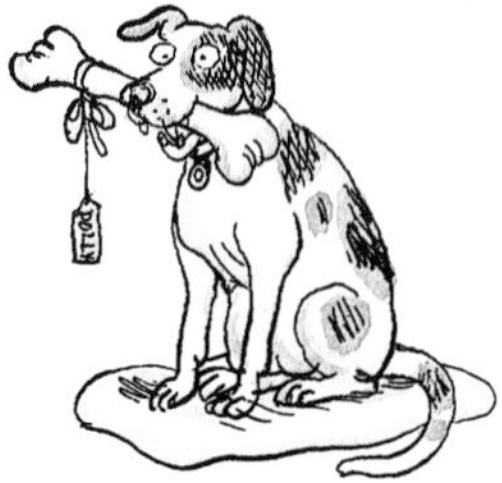

Unwanted Presents

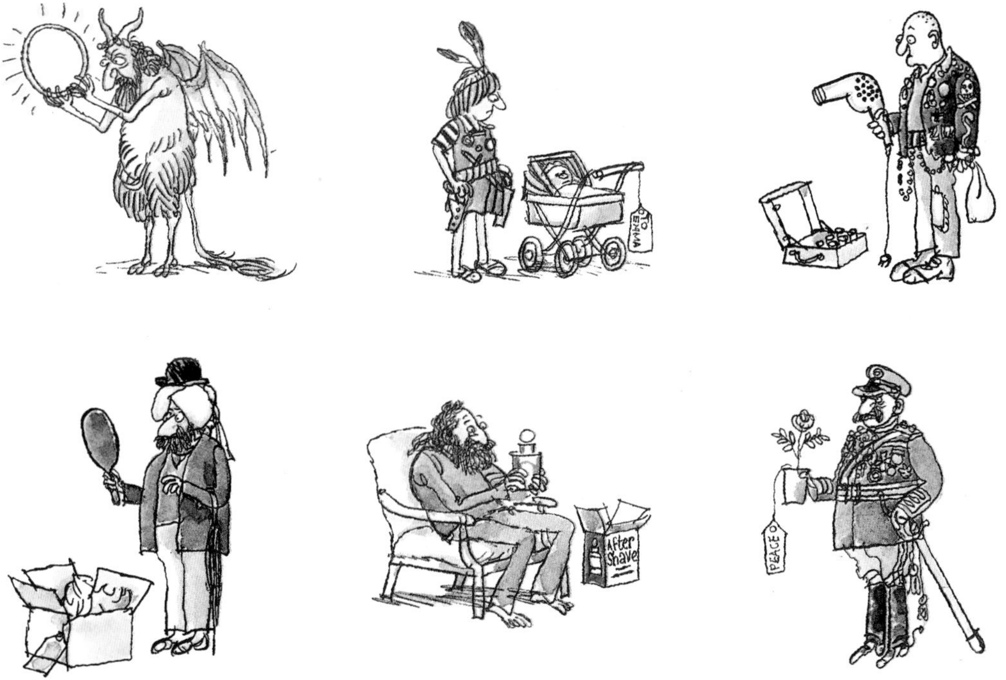
TO EMMA
After Shave
PEACE

THE TWELVE DAYS OF CHRISTMAS

On the first day of Christmas my true love sent to me
A partridge in a pear tree.
On the second day of Christmas my true love sent to me
Two turtle doves and a partridge in a pear tree
On the third day of Christmas my true love sent to me
Three french hens, etc ....
On the fourth day of Christmas my true love sent to me
Four calling birds, etc ....
On the fifth day of Christmas my true love sent to me
Five gold rings, etc ....
On the sixth day of Christmas my true love sent to me
Six geese a laying, etc ....
On the seventh day of Christmas my true love sent to me
Seven swans a swimming, etc. ....
On the eighth day of Christmas my true love sent to me
Eight maids a milking, etc. ....
On the ninth day of Christmas my true love sent to me
Nine pipers piping, etc ....
On the tenth day of Christmas my true love sent to me
Ten drummers drumming, etc ....
On the eleventh day of Christmas my true love sent to me
'leven lords a-leaping, etc ....
On the twelfth day of Christmas my true love sent to me
Twelve ladies dancing, etc ....

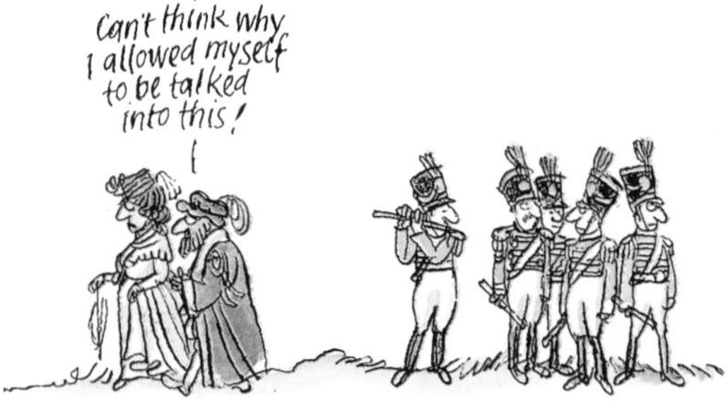
Can't think why I allowed myself to be talked into this!

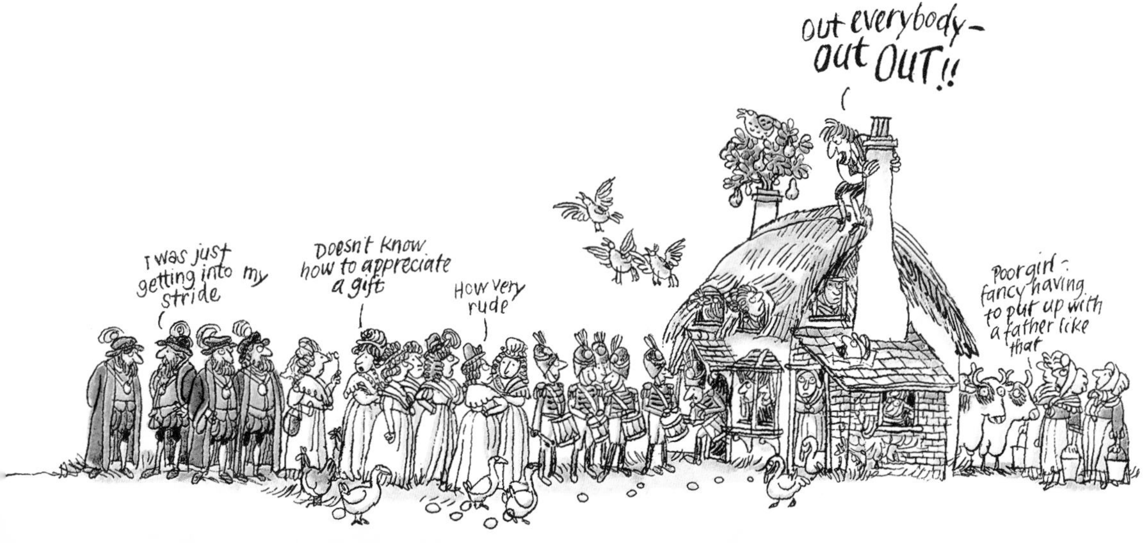
I was just getting into my stride
Doesn't know how to appreciate a gift
How very rude
Out everybody - out OUT!!
Poor girl - fancy having to put up with a father like that

The Seven Deadly Sins

Avarice

Lechery

Pride

Envy

Gluttony

Anger

Sloth

You, sir, are going beyond the joke!
The Seven Virtues
Patience
Faith
Hope
Charity
Justice
Prudence
Forti-tude

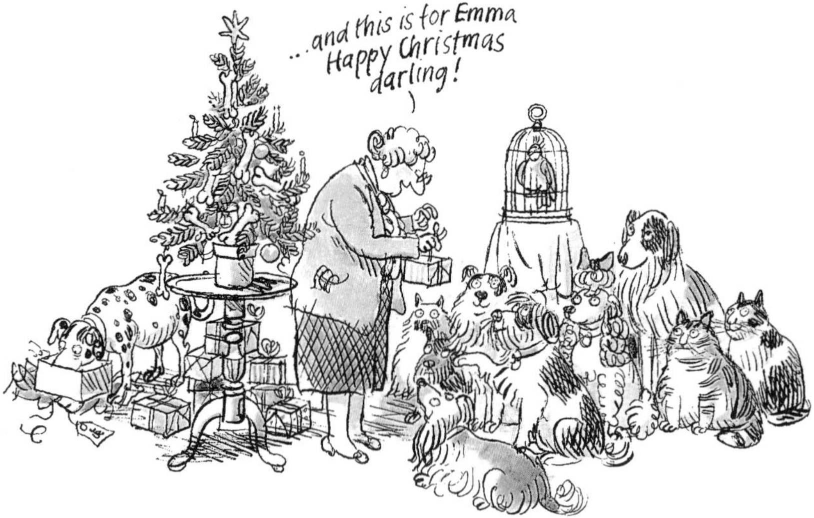
...and this is for Emma
Happy Christmas
darling!

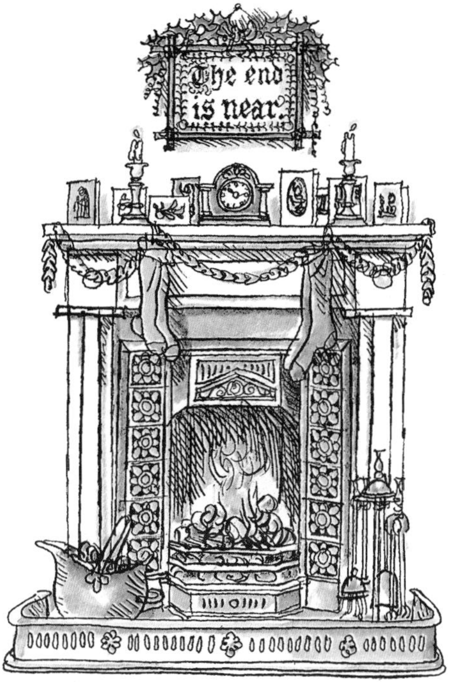
The end
is near

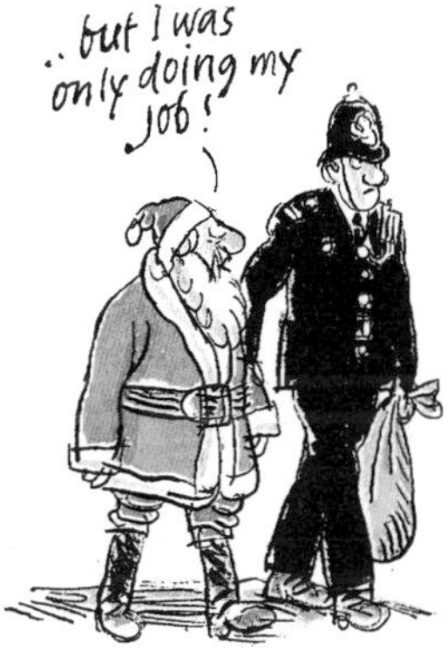
.. but I was only doing my job!

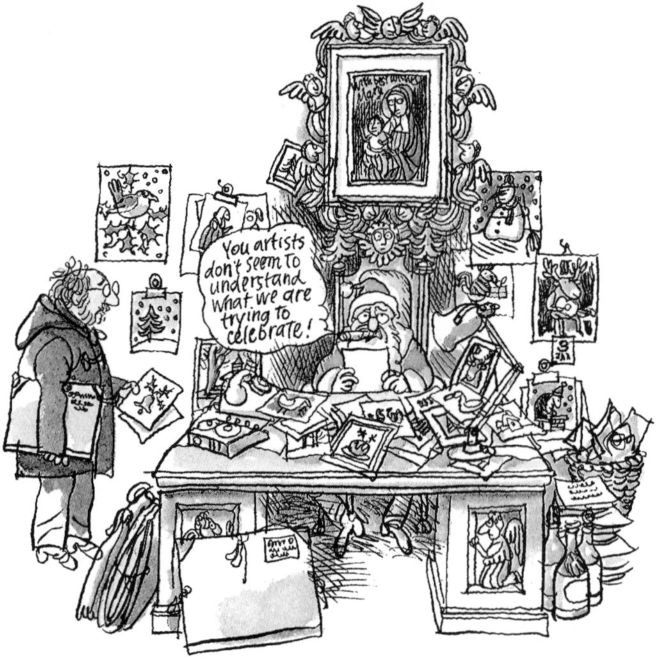
You artists don't seem to understand what we are trying to celebrate!

You and I, my friend, are the symbols of a dying age!

Missionary with highest references, fun loving, enjoys travel, own transport, very generous; wishes to meet lady with broad outlook to share interesting lifestyle

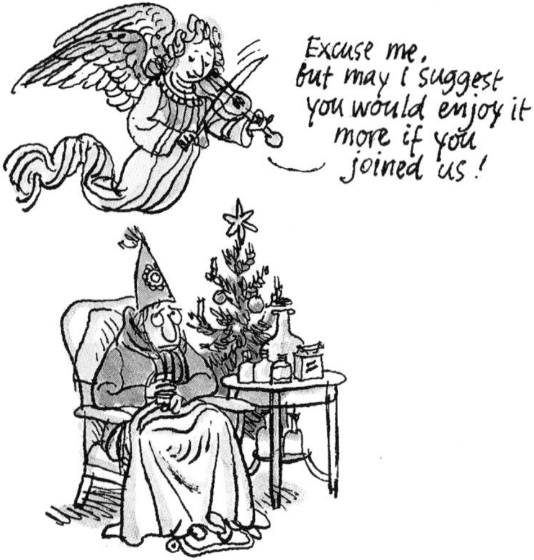
Excuse me, but may I suggest you would enjoy it more if you joined us!

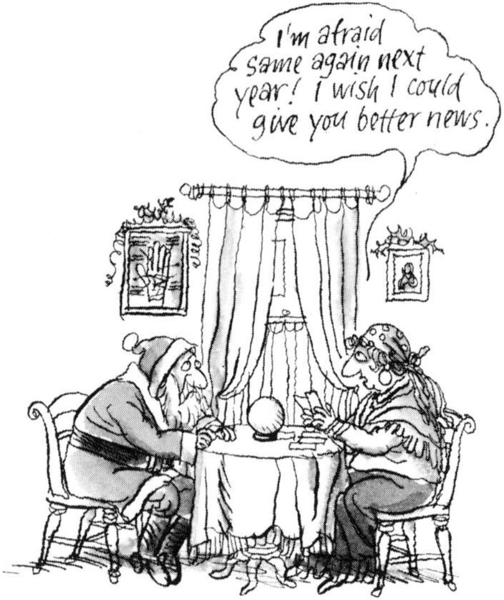
I'm afraid same again next year! I wish I could give you better news.

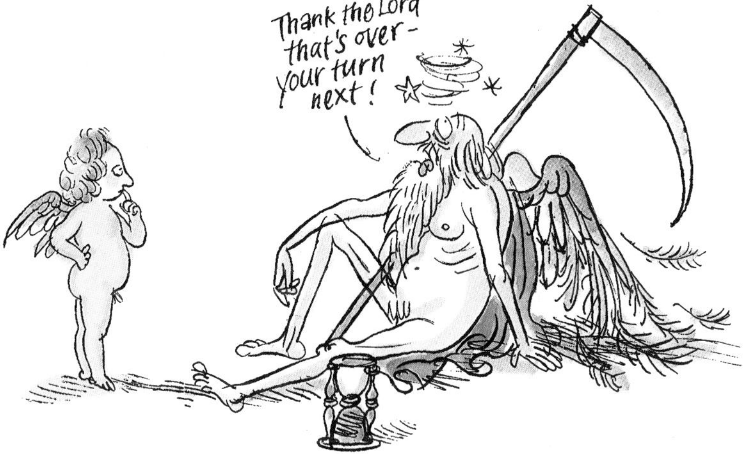
Thank the Lord that's over - your turn next!